What Flies Want

What
Flies
Want

P O E M S

Emily
Pérez

University
of Iowa Press
Iowa City

University of Iowa Press, Iowa City 52242
Copyright © 2022 by Emily Pérez
uipress.uiowa.edu
Printed in the United States of America

Cover design by Susan Zucker
Text design by Omega Clay

Printed on acid-free paper

Library of Congress Cataloging-in-Publication Data
Names: Pérez, Emily (Poet), author.
Title: What Flies Want: Poems / Emily Pérez.
Description: Iowa City: University of Iowa Press, [2022] |
Series: Iowa Poetry Prize
Identifiers: LCCN 2021046125 (print) | LCCN 2021046126
(ebook) | ISBN 9781609388430 (paperback) |
ISBN 9781609388447 (ebook)
Subjects: LCGFT: Poetry.
Classification: LCC PS3616.E74327 W48 2022 (print) | LCC
PS3616.E74327 (ebook) | DDC 811/.6—dc23
LC record available at https://lccn.loc.gov/2021046125
LC ebook record available at https://lccn.loc.gov/2021046126

for my family, my first and best teachers

Contents

The book about violence must be a book of quotations.
For everyone speaks about violence.
Is a book of memories, for everyone's life is riddled.

Julie Carr, from *100 Notes on Violence*

My Son Is

this creature
this bridleless stallion
this sharp-stippled seahorse
   articulating. In my nightmare
  he is screaming
     in the daytime
     he is screaming

the vibration of his lovely body
such furious viability
   rams careening through a tunnel.
   Like a strangler fig
     he hangs upon my limbs
     leaning in to push away. He makes amends
retreating to the quicksand
scaling all the scaffolding
   I can't hold on and my hands are sweaty
   don't come get me

    he'll blind himself, scratch
    his only compass, howl
   in a crowd of sworn-to-silence
stones. In the quiet
  of the evening every rod's
  a loaded gun. I was lucky

    bearing a boy who shot
  straight
    said the things he felt
I was not made for Earth

     his soul beats like a bird
   behind windows. To soothe
   himself he fits his head

below the bedframe, curves
his spine into a crack
beside the hamper.

He made his birthday wish
            to mark himself
        beneath a leafed-out tree
                come true, a thing I will not let
        him do again. He needs

the shock
of a thing done.
Something stronger
        than his anger, something
        forcing fortune out of him.

            He crowds the dark he darks
            into this boyhood wears
                    his hood unhinged.

My Children Use the American Flag

pole
>   as a bayonet

(a handheld flag
>   from a parade

stars and bars
>   cast down to dirt

stick wooden, one foot long
>   gold-painted, pointed cap)

now rubber banded tight
>   and right for lancing

ribs,
>   eyes

too near the barrel
>   of their rifle-style

Nerf gun
>   I have not taught them

"patriot" or "desecrate"
>   or "swords

>   into ploughshares"

Before I Learned to Be a Girl

I used to howl around the eaves,
   a wind unwound. I used to bridle
like a groom atop a stallion, cowing
   pirates into spilling bullion. Never
buckled like a shoe, but shooed the
   shorn beyond the barn so I could hoard
the golden fleece. I fleeced the flock,
   a picky phoenix culling coppers
from their pockets. I pockmarked
   concrete castles with a fist, I frisked
the guards and gunmen. I manned
   the gunwale, gunned down the
siren song until I heard my sternum thrum.
   Wound my way around the Capes
and through canals, threading narrow
   courses like a needle, needling
all my naysayers and needing
   nothing but my own fine fire.

Battle Song

to be performed as a trio with a silent drone

Mom, pretend this is a base.   Pretend
we are in training.   Pretend we are on grass
duty, on rock duty, on hills.   Pretend you cannot
see us.   Pretend that these are real guns.
Pretend that we won't shoot them.
Pretend that we don't hear you
when you say to wait   tell us to stop   please
tell us to stop.   Pretend
we are invisible.   Pretend that we are bad guys
good, no, guys just starting training.   Pretend
the world's at war: war one,   war two,   war ten.
Pretend that we aren't scared.
Pretend that we can stop when it gets dark.
Pretend that we aren't lambs
that we   aren't armed
that we are boys   becoming men
that we are boys   just growing up.

Nightwatch

We killed the mockingbird
and killed so many more. Foolish
to believe that we were ever growing
out of our armored selves, sealed off
like walnuts, small brained and fearful.
We did not want to be vulnerable. We did
not want to stand alone, skin exposed
to the night, trembling against
whatever wind was rising.

Outbound Flight

The young couple
      in the forward row

kiss deep, look through
      the slot

between the 737's
      tight seats, sheepish

before tilting back
      into my lap.

Their armrest
      up. A love before

barriers.

      I never saw

how beautiful we were
      in those early,

harrowed years.
      The thing about privacy

is it narrowed who knew
      what forces

tipped the walls.
      I could count

on one finger
      the people I'd call

in a crisis. A woman
        aligned more closely

with shame
        than gall.

Anniversary

my husband says   *you're married,*
who cares if you are hot by which
he heralds   the   death   of   all
erotics, signals we   will not be
secret   lovers   sneaking   off
the job to grope   each   other's
unknown darknesses in   supply
closets or   family use bathrooms

Your Mood

Your mood is a big balloon that presses the furniture from the room. Your mood has a tailing string that snaps at ankles, angling. Your mood rankles when the spotlight's off, itches when my hands are busy, topples boxes in the basement. I have tried to hold your mood, but like an oiled piglet it squirms free. I bring ice to soothe its mumpsy cheeks. When I punch your mood, I reactivate the yeast. Your mood casts a rain shadow, which I've learned is a place that's neither dark nor feels the rain, two types of comfort I now miss. Your mood is silent in a crowd; under skin it thunder-speaks.

I Want These Problems to Stay Quiet Problems

let no light alight upon this larva
or visit this virus newly named, don't tap
the glass before this adder, attempt to tame
this tempest in an Erlenmeyer flask. Leave lava
in the teapot, steady the tweezer-sculpted bonsai
perched in Tornado Alley
atop a single grain of rice, don't
let anyone ring
the doorbell

My Next Book Is Called

Your Mood

I.

and it's about nights when you
myth morass, this book chronicles
sleep dependent on not
thinking, hooked to a LibriVox recording
of Edward Gibbon's *Decline and Fall*
of the Roman Empire minutes hours
months of decline and fall

II.

and it's about flip
sigh sob grit gnash thrash snap turn
and pull and gasp and then, once full,
float to our son's room to ensure that he'll
absorb your mood

III.

I force field I shield
I turn my cells over
I invisible jet
I bulwark I wrap
myself in this thin
coverlet

My Son Is

Floppy figment
child, fragment frag-
menting. Spending
spineless hours
unrelenting

in a shiver-sway.
Sleepy weepy shimmer-
child, like a feather
floating. Hum
in a windstorm:
wound then gone.

Accoutrements

I wear black to mark our wedding date
the death of all my dreams.
I wear a hood to block periphery,
to muffle, mask, and mute,
as if to say your wailing won't
uproot me. What's the compromise
and how have we endured. Like birds
we bring straw and string and shiny
things to bind the nest, we're best
if we arrive at different times, we're
blessed if you look on us from afar.
I wear this ring: a ribbon, like a scar.

On This Day

On this day I didn't. On this day I did
even though I couldn't. There was no space
for no-saying. On this day I tapped
my reserves, I reserved a tap in the secret
taproom where members keep
their pewter mugs. They let me lie on the stone
floor beneath its sometimes-leaky spout
with my mouth open, a passive pose but
full of hope for some relief. On this day
even the children know not to tread
where I can smell their footsteps.
Their father cries at the table and I fold
and fold bright paper birds.

Today I Wonder What If No One Finds Her

Today a grown girl in the woods, up the hill from Columbine. Today a grown girl head filled up by Columbine. Yesterday a one-way fare, a flight across the nation. The day before a one-way fare. The day before a one-way fare. Every day she plans a trip to Columbine, alerting all the FBI. I'd sacrifice my privacy. I'd sacrifice my right to self-defense. I'd sacrifice my right to a militia. Today a grown girl wearing black and camouflage. One rumor says she's naked. Today will we be hostage to a corpse, a girl with arms, a girl with rights to bear those arms. Today a manhunt for a teenage girl. Today a teenage girl becomes a man who's hunted. Maybe with a wild look. Maybe quiet in the back, as her classmates knew her. Today 400,000 kids stayed home, and mine were fine. Today I told them someone wanted to hurt schools. And the police and principal had talked. And we were safe at home. Today their father told them *crazy woman* and *pump-action shotgun*. Today both kids refused to go run errands. Today they cried when I said *stop acting crazy*. Today they played an online game with guns. Today was like a snow day, only anxious and no snuggles. Today an Uber driver took her up the mountain road. The news report says she hiked through feet and feet of snow. Today my yoga teacher says *where there is chaos, there's a lesson.* Today I tell my older son that *everything's okay* and he replies *there is no time that* everything's *okay.* Today they find her shotgunned near a copse. Today a girl gone in a field. I wonder about what shoes she wore and if her feet felt cold. One day not far away the snow will melt to columbines.

Dinner Conversation

It turns to depression and antidepressants
and I tell them that I—because not all people
with mental illness buy guns or yearn to turn
their pain inside out by shooting in schools—
take one—and this is the dinnertime topic
the thread unspooled from a *why did we not
go to school today* starter—I take an anti-
depressant, and have for two decades—
and it saves me—and one son looks on in awe
or betrayal like I've held keys to the treasure,
like I had a password to the enchanted stone
blocking the cave mouth and didn't tell him
even when oncoming snakes unhinged
their jaws, and he gasps or declares, either way,
it's urgent, regarding the meds:

    I want that

And weeks will pass and we will talk more
before the appointment at which I'm relieved,
or ashamed, or maybe I'm guilty, the mother
who slipped these genes to another, who waited, who
looked at his everyday sorrow as if it were a stage
an age he'd outgrow, that we'd outthink or outsmart
that someday a perfect and quirky quick-witted
friend group would help him turn into film
or a song, abstract art, and when he asks how
the meds work I think back to the book I read
as a teen on a plane, the cover covered because
no one could know my weakness, this shame
of my sad, the book that explained brain chemistry

    the why of me

And years later I'd date briefly
that famous therapist-author's son, *your father meant*
a lot to me, I never said, too afraid of naming my pain,
now to my son I say *there are chemicals in your brain*
that regulate mood—and I too am scared
by the seeming lack of free will this implies,
by hormones in the water, by environmental
decline, by my dependence on pills to live and to thrive,
but despite my strong efforts to levitate
over quotidian grief, the suit that I wore
even in sleep, I could not read or meditate
or yoga pose or swim my way to okay,
nor, as I've watched my husband attempt
now for years, could I think outside the taped walls
of a box of depression, but oh, how those pills
kept me from power washing myself to oblivion
like I did the bird shit on these patio chairs tonight
so we could sit outside for dinner on a late
April evening—

    the Columbine anniversary

a few days out, twenty years since the shooting
that inspired this week's "credible threat" and shuts down
the schools for a day, and my son is learning
about serotonin reuptake inhibitors as I shape
synapses in air with my thumb and index, and I wonder
how I've cursed him, my darling first blessing, and when
I was pregnant, I stopped taking meds on my doctor's
suggestion, then slipped down that drainpipe,
so took them again and re-found my life, yes, this is my true,
my medicated self, and my husband said then, *with us*
as his parents, he'll need them someday,

    why not start early?

And maybe my son is looking up from the well
because I near-drowned him, steeped his fetal brain,
or maybe I tripped him up when I stopped, or maybe
it's luck or a lesson or karma recycling again, and I took
daily meds while pregnant with the second son, this
buoyant one who looks now at us depressive types
in April's fading light and says thoughtfully: *I think
my brain is filled with the silliness*

          chemical,   *and wrapped in flexibility.*

Deciding to Renew Our Vows

That year I took no leave.
We had no rooted story

to use as a foundation for
the shore we'd foundered on.

We'd woven no new myths,
no tapestry made and unmade

every night with thread dipped
in sheep's blood and arrowroot.

We had no bed to serve as pyre,
no new pile of longing,

no inlaid chest of letters,
just a net unraveling.

Each new moon I asked:
When is too late

to reverse a course,
revise a verse.

I imagined entering
our lamplit room

receiving your sighs
as a form of homecoming.

The Door / Locked

Texas summer / one hundred plus heat / again you were / inside the house
/ windows hung with sheets and foil / we had a plan for the future / we
had a plan / for the afternoon / "futuring" / a sign of health / my mother /
your aunt would say / looking to a place / that does not yet exist / imagining
yourself / *congratulations / you made it to another day* / we'd drunk from
the same cup / our family's illness / did not always trust / in future days /
we would slip / into an envelope / of river / slide the sweat-salt off / our
midday skin / let water lick / our inmost sides / untethered / from hands
that usually held / I held / two towels / I have those towels still / ten maybe
fifteen years / some things hold together / no matter how many times /
you use them / outside that door / locked / strewn across the ragged lawn
/ cheatgrass and bull thistle / all your things / books / two by Jane Goodall
/ Carhartts / three clean t-shirts / you did not own much / did not want to
take / up too much space / there was more / a pillow and an army surplus
blanket / a few old photographs / of family / when they used to be / a family
/ and that locked door / I knew you were inside / dying / inside / locked /
we'd angered her / you'd angered her / each day overflowed / its cup of rage
/ I knocked / you'd said no / one would ever love you / I knocked / no one
would love you ever / could not see / beyond those windows / I knocked /
I'd asked what you might say or do / if my man did the things / to me / she
did to you / knocked / she / no one / will ever love / again / you replied /
knocked / I'd kill him / no hesitation / no hyperbole

Aftermath

On the roof, with static on repeat,
I watch as raccoons scour the yard.

The news like a minor chord
in an empty church, hanging.

Today when my students learn
of the shooting, they won't look

up from their books. "In a school?"
one will ask. The world they've grown in.

The night does not feel like December
or respite. More like wet wool

wound tight round my throat. A crash,
and the alley's a riot of garbage.

I envy the scavengers, their trash
into treasure. Their unflinching gaze.

What Flies Want Is Not

what I want
the smoke smell
of the near gone
house the rumble
of storm thrown
down the prairie. What
flies want is left,
forgot, glass rims
where lips touched
last night's fish,
the stain just
setting in carpet.
What I want
is before all that,
the aged cat flicking
her tail, the trail
of sticky melon seeds,
still nestled in the fruit,
the exposed wrist
unadorned with perfume,
the unpierced hunter's catch,
the sealed honey.

How I Learned to Be a Girl

If the beast is unpredictable you must traverse
in postures of submission. Easier to crawl
with your face down toward the earth, nape exposed, expecting
to be struck, which may draw cold contempt, at best compassion.
Fragility may inspire a desire to protect. I learned young to dance
those careful steps around the unexploded mines
where ground was not yet gutted.

Holy, she was, the woman
who stood beside the beast, and I aimed
to be just like her, turning my arrow toward
my chest. I learned the songs that lulled, the charms
that ironed flat the prickling ruff along his neck, the hair that spiked
along his spine when agitated, and when from his sleep guttered a fitful
growl or grinding teeth, I placed, just like a night guard, my careful wrist
inside his mouth.

Primer

I learned my mother's white
tongue, her white words
in white books impressed on crisp
white pages, stories set in white countries
under soft, white snow. I'd never seen snow,
but knew enough to desire its cleansing
cold, its regions where the white-cheeked
damsel with her long, white hair could cede
space to the knight, white on his horse
who whinnied whitely. I'd never ridden a horse,
but knew to fantasize about one, as that's what white
girls did, and even if I never got bedded
by a stable hand or CEO, some tall white man
who could explain things to me, I knew that if I learned
the white language, its syntax and rightness, then,
like a cloud pristine and drifting, I'd be lifted,
I'd look down on my dark home from that unbroken sky.

You Mattered to Me

like a bulwark / like the tie that binds //

You mattered to me like the lion and the lamb //

Like metaphors and meter //

Like the doorway in a dream / like the key to that door / tiny
like the needle's eye / like a rich camel passing through //

Like winter in spring / like lilies with their gold unerring stain //

Like territory claimed //

Like wandering / like walking over desert coals //

Like leaps //

Like the language I first understood to mean you were meaningful / fully
mounted on the mountains / overlooking all the plains //

You planed the planks / you pried the parables / loosed
unwilling tongues / only as damning as the damned deserved //

You danced on the heads of pins I used for holding up my hems //

You hymned / you hummed //

You saved the blood to wet the scraps //

I knew I'd never fool a real god //

With you I had a chance

I Grew Up at the Feet of Unpredictable

practiced at reading turns, shadows
and light around the lips, a quickening
pupil // I study you for clues

when I should have my eyes on the racquetball
its hard polymer whistling toward my cheekbone //
I've only been struck once

by a man who said he would kill himself
if he hurt me again // If he hurt me again
kept score made scars notches

for sideways stumbles // why
have I aimed to please, aligned
my shots, why play any game

      // A roof, a ring
of keys, a precious clutch
of experience, the exchange of love

for money, for blood // Change blood
to money /
to love / to blood

Yes, All Women

on a crowded train and yes
all women and maybe
      it was not okay
      to share upon the sudden
thought this awful thing
that popped to mind
      when a friend mentioned
      that she in an alley
like something else that just
will happen that I like them
      had been and I'm all grown
      and they are girls already
trodden gently down
trodden I said it because
      they've heard it and it will seem
      so far away and then one day
you are and it's like *oh*
this is the way
      it's what's supposed
      to come this time this day
one day one man can make you
a point on a graph
      a number in a bleak brochure one
      man says he ensures his daughters
are protected by not telling them
this day awaits instead
      it comes
      like a bubble burst
no use get used
get used
      to it
      it comes
      it comes
      it comes

How I Learned to [   ]

She said
I must allow his [   ]
to simmer, said
I would not love
myself until I took his [   ]
between my lips
and sucked
until I swallowed [   ]
and held it down
let it digest and circulate
let it pass till all that's left
no more than husk
the scat, the fact
of his un-[   ]
fullness like something
best scraped
from a shoe—
that even my [   ]
stinks
and by for-
giving his, I'd
love mine too.

33

I Have No Right to Speak Because

my scars aren't deep and yet / my smalltown library meeting room / lights
quickoff / elbowcrook to throat / chokeembrace / his skin / severed thick
/ beneath my nails' knives / him screaming *what the hell're you doing?* as if
I / and the jackal pack / Mexico City subway car / power outage trainstop
/ on the tunneltrack / again quickdark / girls as carrion / heatpressed and
teeming / *don't they have motherswivesdaughters?* / power would not / comeon
/ go fly run / latedoors sliding open / San Francisco hillside / Halloween the
Castro / he a queen and maybe hurting / stoned on booze and packoffriends
/ and maybe they were kidhurt all / all scarred and scared / but not everyone
turns scars / quickflip to tentacles / thrashwrap around / what's not theirs

Dear Whiteness,

You dyed all my dreams a deep
white, sang me to white sleep,
spread my peanut butter
on white bread. You taught me
to fill white boxes on a black
background—crossword puzzle words
like "syncope" and "bespoke."
Oh, your boarding schools! Oh,
your long blonde hair and boys
in letter jackets standing on the hoods
of cars! Oh, your school shooters, your white
collar crime! You kept your shirt sleeves
folded, crisp while you grabbed
by the pussy—business casual—
and when your sleeves unfurled you wore
perfect cufflinks. You taught me
to believe in your salad forks, your Watusi,
your grammar books and the back
staircase to which only you have the key,
the one that will lead me to the top.

You are fifteen the first time it happens and you know the power of names
and renaming from your study of the Bible, from learning about slavery,
from that made-for-TV movie about the witness protection program,
and you are no stranger to confusion over your name—you were named
according to family rules: names that sound good in Spanish and English—
but your parents decide to call you by your middle name, your English
name, which results in a lifetime of bureaucratic nightmares including
one time that you will have to sign a legal form verifying that Sarah is the
same as Emily and that you are both those people, and in doctor's waiting
rooms and on the first day of school you've trained yourself to answer to
Sarah even though you feel at best a distant connection to her as if she is a
cousin or alter ego, and at school growing up on the border lots of people
were misnamed, you aren't alone in this, the Mexican teachers would call
Jaime by the masculine, Spanish HY-may instead of what she said, JAY-mee,
making her blush, and in the mouth of the white emcee at football games,
lovely, slender Fátima became FAT-i-ma as she aced grand jetés across the
field when the dance team arrived for halftime, but this time, you are not at
home, you're on your own at boarding school in New Hampshire, a place
as foreign to you as medieval Japan, and why you left home is another story,
but the lesson you learn today is the story that will stick, linger longer than
what you learn in Calculus; no, you are far from South Texas, far from
the town where everyone knows you and your parents and their bicultural
marriage and your siblings and your grandmother who insists she is a citizen,
which she pronounces SEE-tee-zen, and where you move easily across
the segregated streets because in a patriarchal world with a Catholic order
what girl doesn't think of herself as her father's daughter, her family as her
father's line, so now when your new math teacher in this cold classroom
asks you for your last name, your Spanish name, and you say Pérez and think
yourself a Mexican, and she, with a question mark at the end spells Pet-TIS?
and her name is Spruill Kilgore, which for all you know may be common

in this world of duck boots, backward caps, and last names used as first
names, and you respond, no, Pérez, and she responds, oh, you mean PEAR-
ez thereby renaming you, and remember, this is not about witness, it's about
whiteness, this lesson you will learn today, that you are not who you say
you are or think you are, that without your father, your border, without
your family history in this country that predates this country, its lines in
the sand, its river dividers, its *Mayflower*, that here and almost everywhere
in this world that is suddenly a lifetime away from your small hometown
where you are known, she is looking at you, and you are hers, you are theirs
to pronounce.

Song for My Daughter

Because my father pushed me down
      the path alone
Because my bridegroom marked the trail
      with ash
Because a wolf in the woods
      acts not from contempt
      but takes what's his
Because every mouth satisfies
      a body's hunger
Because when asked, I will say
      it was a dream, my love
      a tale I heard
Because the crone hushed and hid me
      while tending her pot
      stewed marrow they'd suckled since birth
Because she was once also a girl
      but hands can form habits
      and recipes spells
      and good mothers feed even their raw, wicked ones
Because with man as my savior
      I was safest alone
Because the bird in the cage
      sang words he had learned
      from the previous girl
Because leashed as she was
      she never said "no"
Because her finger, severed
      continued to sing, and I wanted to use
      its song as my proof
Because a woman's word
      can never be proof
Because I had no wounds on my skin
      when I stumbled home
Because my father slept sound
      on a pillowcase filled

with dowry gold
and I would not wake him
from this particular dream
Because you've heard this before, where boys will be
beasts and girls will be
cloth, torn to ribbons
tied tightly in knots or in bows

Out of the Wood-

work, the girls,
girls at work
in the woods,
whittling, whiling
wood-working girls
girls with awls,
with circular saws,
all at work
like good girls
should:
worked over, worked on,
worked upon,
notched and scored
with a miter's
cross cuts, laced
and latticed,
locked up
all that good girls
withstood.
Out of wood
walked a girl
polished and waxed
lemon scented
scoured smooth,
a girl who reflected
your face
in her shine
a girl well designed
sturdy and fine
sealed shut
like a wardrobe
its wood work
inscribed with girls
in the woods.

Pardon Me, Yes Please, No Thank You

Fear that I will muddle my manners. Fear that I will matter little. Fear that I will dither like a biddie, bobble like a budgie. Fear of being sidelined like a sideshow. Fear of aging, fear of raging, fear of plagiarizing parables. Fear of valuables, of valuing dreck. Fear of being fearful, being feared, of being fearless when my fear would better serve. Fear of being ignorant, imposing, closing down all apertures, of curating suburbia. Fear of verbiage. Fear of loosening the white tongue on my snow-white sneakers, no, the sneak tongue of my snow-white sisters, no, the cis tongue of the norm gifters who say who's what, who's who. Fear of you. Fear of failing all my foremothers of mothering the forefathers of mucking in their mess. Miedo de perder mi niñez. Fear of passing, fear of passing on my passive posture, posturing, of pandering, of putting airs on top of sentiment, fear of sediment cementing.

Accounting

who let you sink // in the sink
of your flesh // the piles and piles // of plush
the forgiveness // in place // of critique // who
let you sleep // when you should // have been
working // awake // who let you shake
loose // like leaves // in the wind // fold into folds
like blankets // like rest // who let you rest
when your best // was just hours // and honing
mere pecking // away // who let you stay
as you are // become more // who // did not
punish // you down // to your core

Please, Whiteness,

I supplicant, compliant
I reliable client. I rely
on rigged possibility. I
plausible deniability.
I culpability. I crane
I cavort. I crapshoot
with the court. I shoot
breezes, breach secrets.
I shifty. I shamble. I
gamble and gambol.
Molly and coddle. I
crawl and I twaddle.
I meek. I model.

Prayer for My White Son

May you never feel
entitled to   May you love
your body but not push
it on another   May you
wonder about
feelings   Find the answers
in a voice   May you know
the power that your
sex and skin pronounce
when you walk in   Dis-
mantle all those shibboleths
that rotten root of power
May you tower over
no one   Seek the rays
of other suns how they fall
on your white skin   May you win
graciously and lose more
often   May you send wishes
paired with work to all
in need   May you bleed
not only for yourself but
for those who stand behind
View all people's suffering
as your own   May you roam
far and wide not hiding
your compassion   May you take
action   Fight until you dis-
cover what is right even
when it means giving up
what you thought you earned
what you thought was right-
and fully yours

At the Hotel Pool

my boys are practicing jumps / one pretends to be Donald Trump / a fool
/ falling unwittingly in / I shush them so as not to offend / the oil and gas
conference attendees / it's happy hour at the poolside bar / the men have
traded slacks / for cargo shorts / dry-cleaned shirts with ties / for Polos
with the collars raised / like the preppy stars / of my teenage dreams / all
grown up / thinning hair / beer bellies / financial sense plus jostling /
off-color jokes / mixed company / one woman for every cluster / keeping
pace / breezy bluster / watered-down margaritas / plastic cups / women still
done up / linen pants / silk shirts / salon-blown hair / a man picks one up /
because he can / makes a show of will-he / won't-he / throw her in / he does
/ then joins her / splash! / an onlooker whoops / my boys are confused / the
doused woman / bites a smile on her face / to show she respects / this oaf /
her boss? / he eyes the skin-slick top / her designer bra / she will not fuss /
makes a wave or two / she can't leave the pool / for half an hour / until some
dry man thinks / to bring her a towel / her beige outfit / now see-through /
some men look sidewise / more of a show / she's still their colleague / needs
them to know / her mind / the boyman pulls off his soaking shirt / throws it
at another man / nonplussed / trying to escape the poolside bar / the bomb
almost hits / my six year old / I turn and say / not a word / these are men /
who rule the world / the men / I try not to offend / lest one picks me up /
here / in front of my sons / and throws me down

Once I Learned to Be a Girl

Once upon a time there was a little box,
a wooden vessel filled with tiny wants.

Once upon a time the box was buried,
the map and key tucked high upon a shelf.

And when her hands were free she cut
and colored, drew straight lines and crafted

a trim house. Then she turned a needle round.
She teased herself into a net.

She threw herself into the street to wait.
The one she caught she placed inside

the house. She carved the rooms and roof
to fit his moods. Over time she learned

to drown her thoughts, to put her book
aside when he walked in. Once,

she lay down flat, became a mirror,
a silvered glass in which he saw himself.

She learned to tidy, to arrange. Keep everything
in order. Once while tidying she came

across a map that she'd forgot,
a map that led her to a buried box.

And when she found the key and looked inside,
whatever had been buried there had died.

Rose Moon

I lipstick all my face.
I can be your best-your-student-girlfriend-mom.
My husband does not know the game of placate.
He plays the game of get along and go along.
He broods manly or he laughcoughs at the halftime score
while I purr in the corner. Arching all my vertebrae like vowels.
Licking all your papercuts.
Easing your disease.
I titter like a teakettle and knit a compromise,
my position compromising.
I serve spoonfuls from the new-glued sugar bowl.

When You Balance

on the shovel's
wedge, its blade a seesaw
axe, when you hit your head

on concrete, falling off
the bench, these acts
of accidental self- humili-

mutilation, when your spirit calls
for something new-created
sirens us all

toward the burning boy.
Do I recognize those flames?
Who calls a fire by its name?

When He Comes

And he will come.
          He will be one of ours
hardened in the forge

of dinner tables
          and bedtime stories.
He'll have shot up

like a sapling
          grown drunk under
his personal sun and purified

water, a boy in man's armor
          arms and hands grasping
at what's his to master

his to grope and to finger
          like soft bills in a fold.
To hunt and to have and to hold

in a headlock.
          His to plunder.
His to shiver and shake.

He will quiver
          his arrow into the fray.
He will come for us

from us. Wrung
          from our own worship-
ful hands.

Lockdown, 1st Grade

Mom, we had to hide
Mom, it was a game

It wasn't like a normal game
The man outside was hunting

The man outside was seeking
The teacher turned out all the lights

and we did hugs and bubbles
Hugs around ourselves and bubbles in our mouths

We could not let them pop
We did not make a peep We curled up

just like this in balls beside the cubbies
We were chickens in a nest no we were babies

in their eggs We watched the crack
under the door to see his feet We listened

for his legs to walk   And when we heard we held
our breath We held it for a long time

It wasn't like the last time
The teacher told us if we won

we'd get a prize we'd celebrate
But she forgot   and we just got to breathe

My Son Is

porous / a sponge / when detritus is stirred / did you know the word
flotsam / can refer to a person / a vocabulary book / taught me / another
name / inhumane / a metaphorical knife / for wounding the foe / my
son is permeable / penetrable / he has leeched up the screeching / from
downstairs / from upstairs / outdoors / words we lobbed in his sleep /
what's seeped in his pores / his cells realigned / with the way we maligned /
he resonates / shakes with our hateful / hums with our dirge

I Wanted a Full Dose of Never-Mind of Not-Ever-

will-I never-again not now and not endeavoring to
please turn your gaze to another thing less
alarming, I did not want unsettling, the pit in the grip
of the stomach's clenched fist, the wrench in the works
of the mason's bricks laid like a table set but the guest
not arriving, driving out into the rain
to call the lost dog we've known only weeks he wrecks
our sleep with responsibility, I wanted no last will
and wishes, no testament unturned, unearned. I wanted soothe
and settle, no nettle in the pudding, no pull in the stocking,
no pecking pullet waiting for the axe to fall. I wanted full
and saturated, un-curious, abated, tucked and trimmed,
no hem unsightly, no nightly news, no wedge issue, no ledge.

Today's Arc

today's art.
Today's swift

anger arrowing.
I thought
of your pain but not

of salve or suture.
I rely on the expert
to say it's time to stop.

My heart. Your heart.

Boding

Looking back, we did not know
        which sign came first:
                The roosters roosting on the roof
        refusing to touch ground.
Horses snorting in their stalls
        pupils, nostrils widening.
                The goat atop the cow's back.
        The hound dog keening on the porch,
scratching at the open door.
        The red kites gathering.
                The bloody caul that cloaked the foal.
        Fragments from the teapot's shattered spout.
The knife that scarred the sideboard.
        The memory box, the cradle cracked.
                The letters used for kindling.
        The stars lined up like dead men's eyes.
The dried up well.
        The weeping oak.
                The moon, low and waning.
        The feeling of familiar hands
upon the throat, contracting.

Hindsight: Part III

Because I wanted to keep
        appearances, because I was ashamed
of your loud avowals, flapping hands.
        Because of agitate and irritate.
Because nothing could fill me.
        I was tending toward more
emptiness, my guts a breath
        away from retching up regrets.
The wretched man his wretched wife
        their wretched ever after. I heard
you shouting in the alley. I heard
        shooting in the alley and thought
of you. I heard your moaning mouth
        howl for help and then you bit
my hand; you poisoned all
        the garden. Because you ratcheted
the recklessness, the tension
        hard to hold. Because you wrenched
my wrists while I hung on.

You Have All Day

to be good to yourself—
        I have only this
corner with no desk
           —you can dip your toes
in the clear hum, the strum and thrum
        of energymatter, you can meditate
on meaning—I am in a forced
        mediation, having crossed
a real warlock, my hands cursed—
        you read scriptures and unearth your past—
I censor, critique and click off boxes of done,
        I have a lamp but only one outlet
I toggle my devices—you remodel
        rooms to accommodate
your instruments—I get paid
        to pay you to take care
so your happiness can play
        a starring role in our family
drama—it's better this way, when I'm
        the martyr, when I'm in control.

After Watching the Vampire Movie

The blood
　　　bursts and blusters
from my child's head.
　　　He's got a cloth
bright red, attached,
　　　apologetic that he couldn't
find a dirty rag
　　　to catch the iron-tinged
fountain flowing
　　　from his nose. He goes
from my threshold
　　　to the dark, afraid
to be seen, to see my face,
　　　its confirmation
of the quantity, he paces
　　　just outside my room.
It's midnight or more
　　　and his father's asleep
after giving up
　　　on so many things.
I recognize the shame
　　　in my son's small voice
the fear of what's befallen
　　　and I pull myself up
from the depths
　　　I was treading
to usher this creature,
　　　no longer soft like a child
but pointed and edged,
　　　to the tiled bathroom.

Shirtless, he's striped
　　　bright lines down his chest
his face a miracle
　　　of red. He whimpers.

I stroke his back
        with my free hand,
with the other I place
        compress after compress
against his nose. Blood
        comes in ropes and spurts
like oil paints from a tube.
        I cannot catch them
fast enough. At last
        they start to slow.

He wants a bath, but I
        make him shower first
not wanting him to steep in the pink
        of his own hot life.
He wants me near, and I press
        the softening crust
off his cheeks, I help him scrub
        his hands. In the tub
he relaxes into modesty
        but stops me as I leave,
may he sleep on the floor
        in my room. I gather blankets
and say I'll see him soon.
        The other child stirs, wants to eat
an egg, and joins us.

This is the part of the poem
        where I should meditate
on being a mother
        awake in the night
tending to two not-quite-boys
        who still need her touch
but as I write, my husband's awoken
        in full-blown lurch,
quaking over hurts
        from the past. When I reach
out to him, he roars. Wounded,

a tiger in a cage of his own design,
so many reasons why
      he cannot stanch the flow.
This is the part of the poem,
      as in life, where two children
are still asleep on my floor
      and my husband rages
alone. I'm tired of caring
      and caring for.

Every Man's a Ticking Bomb

potential energy
and harm
harnessed—just
a hair
trigger. If you read this

you will find my words
unfair.
If you read this
you will say that I ignored
the wall I am
the way I light
the fuse. Just now

you appeared
in this dark room
having read
not this scrawl
but the scowl
on my face
and proclaimed
When I get tense
you treat me like your dad
treats your mom.

Every man's a ticking bomb.

Vows

I will not muddle in mediocrity. I will not be
mid-range or mid-level. I account for no one.
I assist myself up the ladder. I
call for the bucket and udder, milk
my own damn cows, and churn what's pumped.
I'm sorry, my darling, I will not be treed
or stumped by your meteorics. I'm
skating by in my glittery skirt, waving.

When You Slipped into the Lake

I didn't feel it coming the gathering of fishing rods and water shoes did
not portend a sinking or upending. In fact our child's jumping on a couch
backed up against a half-wall, overlooking the steep drop to the basement
rang out more disaster, his laughter, taunting me each time he flew up
and almost over, in it the wave of pain that would ink wash all our future
making me responsible though I'd caught his every breath, mapped his every
step, foretold his bowel's every move, unthinkable that I would not foresee,
forswear and ward off danger as I'd learned to think five steps ahead and
plan, gather heat blankets and beans in cans. Already I had worked out my
new life, the flat I'd take, the way I'd keep the child undetected. And when
the sun went down behind the hills and you did not return, no glint of a
red canoe atop the lake's unspeaking face, no Poseidon risen from the deep
to redeem a curse he'd laid, and your truck still in the driveway, it came as a
surprise, the foresight that I'd stored so well, fed myself so carefully. What
had it revealed but a bellyache? I'd been testing wind and watching ground
for the route your feet would take, when in front of me the earth had just
unbirthed you, relinked you to her omphalos, sucked you down before I
earned a win with my escape.

Ten Years Later My Husband Walks Out of the Woods

after "Hans My Hedgehog"

In one version you remove your coat
of quills at dusk, drape it by the hearthside.

My father's bravest men then burst
into our room and net the carapace, fling

it in the waiting blaze, burn the thorns
that stippled you. The hollow spires

in the fire sing like copper smelted,
the slag amassing on the flagstones

cooling to a twisted fist of all that had you
hinged. Unmasked at last you stand

before me, born anew: not a monster, not
a man, but a fledgling flayed. Oh husband,

what soulbrave bargain have you made
that leaves you so tender, and how

am I to salvage you?—just wife, not
witch, not doctor.

Stolen Things: Part III

I stole the necklaces and then the earrings   soon   I had scads
and scads of stolen things   a cascade of icy waterfalls   adorning

my mother harbored the painting   beneath the bed,   *The Louvre*
imprint   what did she know

about the woman, the man,   collateral that can't be sold,
the request to hold   onto this—for a while—just until   the woman

could make her break   be broken

one cannot wear the stolen thing
    except in secret   twirling

        before a darkened mirror

what else under the bed: the rifle   the things we rifled through
a careful girl   I knew   every coin   the teeth

the fairy plucked   marbles in a Mason jar   I knew
the pocketknife, the guitar strings   the smell of all those secrets

and what good is a secret   except to fester all your gut

my children rifle: we decide to give their dad a skateboard
and my youngest bursts   *I know where to find one!*   leads me

to the closet, where   I'd hidden it just days before

now the guns in my aging parents' house   unlocked unloaded
or locked and loaded   or   waiting   to explode

in my hide-and-seek sons' finding hands

and when a friend steals his magic wand my son cries
　　　　but does not begrudge　　　　the wish for magic

I know I need to return the jewelry　　　but it buds in my hands
　　　　my prints shimmer　　　　　　　with someone's DNA

there is a man walking in my yard　　　　leaving footprints in the snow

my son cannot believe we own such a big tree　　　do we own a tree

the pear sapling we bought and planted
　　　　the spruce and pines stretch a century

I say *we will not take it with us if we leave*

from whom was this land stolen

I put my hand on my son's bare back *mine, he's mine*

Second-Grade Drop-Off

puffy-coated kids pock the blacktop
pinging like bumper cars // my breath shallows

when I hear a man say *here is where*
they congregate // as if for prayer // as if fish

barreltrapped // the bell alarms
and teachers hustle them indoors

I scan the schoolyard // let my breath out

whose life is shield enough
to save my boy // or anyone

each day at school a first grader
calls my boy *weak* // a coach reports

today was good: this time no tears //
at home my son counts cash // saving

up to buy a bright-orange plastic
pump-action rubber-tipped foam-

bullet shooting gun

Darling, I Would Never // That I'd Ever Want

you to be something other
than // what kind of mother
asks for change // calls it growth
looks on imperfections and picks //
seeks to pour cement // fill the gaps
with some fixture or fixative // what kind
of mother asks her love to bend // fit
into a stricture // structures futures based on
// what makes her want to teach
that lesson // lessen love by asking
for a shift // what kind of woman. I'm it.

My Son Is

did you know the night before your diagnosis
we had a break-in, and when I woke, the door
was open to the morning, just

barely light, screen door swung out, front door
swung in, and the jackets on the sofa
like the coat tree'd dropped a limb

raincoat pockets out like tongues
and an iron latch knocked off
the giant chest in the living room

papers leaf-littered the floor, blown
as if a whirlwind had stirred just this side
of the entry, what else had been altered

(after the first break-in the police told me to throw
my things away to buy new
things that I wouldn't want to think

about hands on things) the night
of the break-in, the night before
your diagnosis, your father rattled

awake and sloughed downstairs,
he'd fallen asleep in your brother's bed,
and perhaps the bunk frame's moan alarmed

whatever spirit had tried
our door, knowing we were careless, open
to rummage, whatever'd shifted our entrance, swept

out again, and sometimes you leave
a door open and sometimes someone decides
to try the handle and sometimes we

don't swaddle what needs
cradling, and then we went to the doctor
already cracked, spilled everything

Underground /

In the cemetery / by your old house / I choose a fox / a fox
occurs to me to lead / because fantastic / phantom / totem / slip and slink
but the fox resists / and Sarah's there / your dog who shares my name

she's smiling / loveful / playful / as she always was / caring / more
than needing caring for / and what I really want / someone to care / more
than needing / caring for

somewhere safe / I try to follow / into that culvert / the place she'd chase
a ball or squirrel / under the road between / two banks / she won't go or / I
won't go or / we won't go together / and I'm on a cliff / the one we hiked

those days when I wrote / and you still loved / who you were / though
messed up in some other ways / and me afraid / we'd run out of words
I jump / and everything is rose / creamy dreamy / and sky periphery

trying to bring down / all my walls / and if I / should I / and first up
is the walled woman / and next is the man whose nerves are sleeves
whose entrails shake / your hand / the last is the boy / now a man

I first met when our baby grew / in me / and our child is five / and what
has grown / between us / and words / stretch out / faces / drawn
with white chalk / a wall in a basement / a theater / and how did I get / first

left then right / then backward / called backward / where two faces
and I'm still judging / me / I'm well / I'm doing / I'm doing well / I'm good
I'm good at doing / and how do I feel / how did I feel / relaxed / relaxed or

the waves and waves and waves
make me okay / I pray / enough / make me enough / always
been everything / or tried to be

Tonight When They Try On My Bra

the little one crushes the cups, testing
       their air, as if the garment
will fill with fantasy. He wants the straps
       and fastenings, he wants
the silky armor girding
       his six-year-old skin. His chest
shimmers with laughter. Their father
       breathing down the stairs. I shout
a half truth to the stairwell before
       he's in the door. I'm half sure
of what he'll do. Some men
       would meet the sight with fists
others with shame, he cocks half
       a smile, as if to say
what did he expect
       leaving his boys alone
       with such a woman.

I Have Plenty

I have a house full of sons.
I have a home full of swords.
I have real armor and fake
vulnerability, I have my work
cut out and my art cut out
and my secret cutout
heart in the shape of a string
of hand-clasped paper dolls
folded over each other, waiting.
I have pleasures: outright
admiration for words. I have
sunlight dappling an unshake
able sense of my own self-worth
that sprang from my father's self
ishness my mother's bow-down.
I have a dearth of role models
but love and belief in my bound
aries, inviolable my voice
can be powerful, I have things
to unlearn I have wealth
unearned I have privilege
to spare I have breathable
air, not sure for how long
given how I contribute
to destruction of Earth. I have
love for all people except
I have foes. I have quest
ions I have doubts in the reach
of my arms in my self-right
eousness. I have a body I alt
ernately praise and despise do I
see through my needs am I
desiring or just aiming as always
to please do I find myself re
quiring—no—I have plenty.

Notes & Acknowledgments

"Accoutrements" was inspired by a conversation between Ira Glass and Alain de Botton on *This American Life*, in the episode "Choosing Wrong." "Battle Song" is a found poem in the words of W.A.M. and F.F.M. "Dinner Conversation" and "Today I Wonder What If No One Finds Her" draw from the events of April 17, 2019, when a teenager traveled from Florida to Colorado based on her obsession with the massacre at Columbine High School twenty years earlier. She purchased a gun shortly after arriving in Colorado. Her actions, deemed a "credible threat" by the FBI, shut down hundreds of schools in the Colorado Front Range for the day while the police searched for her. She was found dead by suicide on April 18 in the mountains near Denver. "The Door / Locked" is for M.A.C. "Lockdown, 1st Grade" is a found poem in the words of W.A.M. "Song for My Daughter" draws from Project Gutenberg's version of the story "The Robber Bridegroom," as collected by the Brothers Grimm. "Ten Years Later My Husband Walks Out of the Woods" draws from Project Gutenberg's version of the story "Hans My Hedgehog," as collected by the Brothers Grimm.

More people than I can name here helped nurture this book.

Thank you to James McCoy, Tegan Daly, Karen Copp, Susan Hill Newton, Allison Means, and the team at the University of Iowa Press. Thank you to judge Brenda Shaughnessy for believing in these poems.

Sasha West, thank you for your intellect, generosity, cheerleading, and heart at all stages of this project.

Nancy Reddy, thank you for being a friend and collaborator.

David Campos, thank you for your excellent advice on genre and ordering.

Jenny Tran, thank you for your eye, your mood boards, and above all, your friendship.

Jill McEldowney and Madhouse Press, thank you for publishing *Made and Unmade*, the chapbook at the heart of this book.

Thank you to the Ledbury Emerging Critics mentors Sarah Howe, Sandeep Parmar, and Vidyan Ravinthiran for pushing my writing and opening doors.

Thanks also to the Ledbury US cohort, Mario Chard, Abraham Encinas, and Shamala Gallagher. You all kept me writing through a pandemic; I'm excited to see what's in store for us on the other side.

Thanks to Angela Narciso Torres and the folks at *RHINO Reviews*—you also kept me writing; to CantoMundo and Letras Latinas for sustained support and community; to all the folks at Community of Writers, where some of these poems were born; to my employer, Colorado Academy, for valuing work/life balance and supporting me as a writer; to all the childcare providers, doctors, and therapists who have supported my family and me; to vaccine makers, distributors, and public health officials who have supported us all.

Thanks to friends and inspirations: Francisco Aragón, Rosebud Ben-Oni, Erin Cantos, Anthony Cody, James P. Davis, Camille Dungy, Carolina Ebeid, Carmen Giménez Smith, Celeste Guzmán-Mendoza, Meg Hill, Katy Hills, Jodie Hollander, Julie Irons, Jenn Kao, Ali Kittle, Nina McConigley, Jill Meyers, Wayne Miller, Keya Mitra, Amanda Nowlin-O'Banion, Kate O'Donnell, Deborah Paredez, Sylvia Park, Mónica Parle, Khadijah Queen, Laura Sandbloom, Liza Skipwith, Carolina Treviño, Jeanine Walker, Elaine Walters, Kathy Williams, Elissa Wolf-Tinsman, Sarah Wright, and Tiphanie Yanique.

Thanks to my parents, Rudy and Margaret, for believing in me. Extra special thanks to you, Mom, for all your help with childcare. Thanks to more beloved family: Linda, Joe, Margot, John, Lorrie, Sarah, Karen, Mary, Larry, Edward, David, Lorena, Octavia, Federico, Ileana, John, Janowyn, Hayden, and Ridge.

Matt, my thanks to you for walking out of the woods, for partnering through a pandemic, for parenting two beautiful children, for committing to the work, for tolerating my stress, for loving me anyway, for valuing my writing (even the stuff about the husband), for making music always, and for cooking delicious food.

Wylan and Felix, this book is full of glimpses of each of you when you were younger than you are now, reading this. This book is full of my love and fear poured into outlines shaped like you; full of combinations, inflations, and imaginations of you. But this book does not capture the astonishing truths of you. Thank you for all the ways you teach me every day, for the joy you bring to my life, and for your wish in a rose garden wishing well.

Grateful acknowledgment to the journals where these poems have appeared, sometimes in previous versions or under slightly different names: *The Acentos Review* ("Aftermath," "Lockdown, 1st Grade," "When He Comes"), *ANMLY* ("You Mattered to Me"), *Barrow Street* ("Your Mood"), *Botticelli* ("Accounting," "Accoutrements," "Anniversary," "Deciding to Renew Our Vows"), *Copper Nickel* ("The Door / Locked"), *Cosmonauts Avenue* ("Pardon Me, Yes Please, No Thank You"), *CutBank* ("Today I Wonder What If No One Finds Her"), *Diode* ("Hindsight: Part III," "Nightwatch," "Once I Learned to Be a Girl" [as "Making and Unmaking"]), *Fairy Tale Review* ("Out of the Wood-," "Song for My Daughter"), *Harpur Palate* ("Please, Whiteness,"), *The HIV Here and Now Project* ("Boding"), *Iron Horse Literary Review* ("My Children Use the American Flag," "Second-Grade Drop-Off"), *Letras Latinas* ("C~~orrección~~ / Correction"), *Missouri Review* ("Ten Years Later My Husband Walks Out of the Woods"), *Poetry Northwest* ("Outbound Flight"), *Prairie Schooner* ("I Wanted a Full Dose of Never-Mind of Not-Ever-," "My Son Is" [as "My Son Is This Creature"]), *RHINO* ("Before I Learned to Be a Girl"), *Silk Road Review* ("What Flies Want Is Not"), *Tin House* ("Primer"), *Queen Mob's Teahouse* ("My Son Is," "Stolen Things: Part III"). "Yes, All Women" was anthologized in *Latinas: Struggles & Protests in 21st Century USA*. *Made and Unmade*, a chapbook containing several of these poems, was published by Madhouse Press in 2019.

1987
Elton Glaser, *Tropical Depressions*
Michael Pettit, *Cardinal Points*

1988
Bill Knott, *Outremer*
Mary Ruefle, *The Adamant*

1989
Conrad Hilberry, *Sorting the Smoke*
Terese Svoboda, *Laughing Africa*

1990
Philip Dacey, *Night Shift at the Crucifix Factory*
Lynda Hull, *Star Ledger*

1991
Greg Pape, *Sunflower Facing the Sun*
Walter Pavlich, *Running near the End of the World*

1992
Lola Haskins, *Hunger*
Katherine Soniat, *A Shared Life*

1993
Tom Andrews, *The Hemophiliac's Motorcycle*
Michael Heffernan, *Love's Answer*
John Wood, *In Primary Light*

1994
James McKean, *Tree of Heaven*
Bin Ramke, *Massacre of the Innocents*
Ed Roberson, *Voices Cast Out to Talk Us In*

1995
Ralph Burns, *Swamp Candles*
Maureen Seaton, *Furious Cooking*

1996
Pamela Alexander, *Inland*
Gary Gildner, *The Bunker in the Parsley Fields*
John Wood, *The Gates of the Elect Kingdom*

1997
Brendan Galvin, *Hotel Malabar*
Leslie Ullman, *Slow Work through Sand*

1998
Kathleen Peirce, *The Oval Hour*
Bin Ramke, *Wake*
Cole Swensen, *Try*

1999
Larissa Szporluk, *Isolato*
Liz Waldner, *A Point Is That Which Has No Part*

2000
Mary Leader, *The Penultimate Suitor*

2001
Joanna Goodman, *Trace of One*
Karen Volkman, *Spar*

2002
Lesle Lewis, *Small Boat*
Peter Jay Shippy, *Thieves' Latin*

2003
Michele Glazer, *Aggregate of Disturbances*
Dainis Hazners, *(some of) The Adventures of Carlyle, My Imaginary Friend*

2004
Megan Johnson, *The Waiting*
Susan Wheeler, *Ledger*

2005
Emily Rosko, *Raw Goods Inventory*
Joshua Marie Wilkinson, *Lug Your Careless Body out of the Careful Dusk*

2006
Elizabeth Hughey, *Sunday Houses the Sunday House*
Sarah Vap, *American Spikenard*

2008
Andrew Michael Roberts, *something has to happen next*
Zach Savich, *Full Catastrophe Living*

2009
Samuel Amadon, *Like a Sea*
Molly Brodak, *A Little Middle of the Night*

2010
Julie Hanson, *Unbeknownst*
L. S. Klatt, *Cloud of Ink*

2011
Joseph Campana, *Natural Selections*
Kerri Webster, *Grand & Arsenal*

2012
Stephanie Pippin, *The Messenger*

2013
Eric Linsker, *La Far*
Alexandria Peary, *Control Bird Alt Delete*

2014
JoEllen Kwiatek, *Study for Necessity*

2015
John Blair, *Playful Song Called Beautiful*
Lindsay Tigue, *System of Ghosts*

2016
Adam Giannelli, *Tremulous Hinge*
Timothy Daniel Welch, *Odd Bloom Seen from Space*

2017
Alicia Mountain, *High Ground Coward*
Lisa Wells, *The Fix*

2018
Cassie Donish, *The Year of the Femme*
Rob Schlegel, *In the Tree Where the Double Sex Sleeps*

2019
William Fargason, *Love Song to the Demon-Possessed Pigs of Gadara*
Jennifer Habel, *The Book of Jane*

2020
Emily Pittinos, *The Last Unkillable Thing*
Felicia Zamora, *I Always Carry My Bones*

2021
Emily Pérez, *What Flies Want*